D1385356

WILD RACERS

Bob Woods

This edition first published in 2010 in the United States of America
by Marshall Cavendish Benchmark.

Marshall Cavendish Benchmark
99 White Plains Road
Tarrytown, NY 10591
www.marshallcavendish.us

Library of Congress Cataloging-in-Publication Data
Woods, Bob.
Wild racers / by Bob Woods.
p. cm. — (Racing mania)
Summary: "Provides comprehensive information on the history, the famous
faces, the design, and the performance of the amazing machines behind wild
racers"—Provided by publisher.
Includes bibliographical references and index.
ISBN 978-0-7614-4389-6
1. Motor vehicles—Juvenile literature. 2. Racing—Juvenile literature.
3. Transportation—Juvenile literature. 4. Speed—Juvenile literature.
I. Title.
TL147.W68 2010
796.7—dc22
2009003169

Cover: Photolibrary
Half Title: Chase Jarvis/Corbis
P4: Jeff Strauss/iStockphoto; P5: landrea/Dreamstime; P6-7: Bugatti Trust; P7: Bettmann/Corbis; P8-9:
Duomo/Corbis; P9 Duomo/Corbis; P10-11: Paul Spinelli/Getty Images; P11: Paul Spinelli/Getty Images;
P12-13: Getty Images Sport/Getty Images; P13: auto imagery Inc; P14-15: www.MMRAracing.com; P15: www.
MMRAracing.com; P16-17: Rick Walker; P17: Stephen Coburn/Shutterstock; P18: landrea/Dreamstime; P19: landrea/
Dreamstime; P20: Fox Photos/Hulton Archive/Getty Images; P21: Photolibrary; P22-23: Jens-Ulrich Koch/AFP/Getty
Images; P24: First Light/Getty Images; P25: Uniqueglen/Dreamstime; P26-27: Chase Jarvis/Corbis; P28: W. Perry
Conway/Corbis; P29: Jeff Vanuga/Corbis; P30-31: Scott McDermott/Corbis; P31: Shutterstock; P32: Richard Hamilton
Smith/Corbis; P33: Brian Bahr/Getty Images; P34: Andreas Gradin/Alamy; P35: Stefan Aufschnaiter/Sports & News/
Reuters;P36: Tony Tremblay/iStockphoto; P37: Tony Tremblay/iStockphoto; P42: Bryn Williams/Reuters;
P43: Associated Press; P44: Jon Nicholson/McLaren via Getty Images; P45: Associated Press.

Created by Q2AMedia
Series Editor: Jim Buckley
Art Director: Sumit Charles
Client Service Manager: Santosh Vasudevan
Project Manager: Shekhar Kapur
Designer: Joita Das and Prashant Kumar
Photo research: Shreya Sharma

Printed in Malaysia

135642

CONTENTS

INTRODUCTION

Wild racers include many weird, wacky machines, from Go-Peds to snowmobiles that race on water!

Racing has been around as long as people have. We started off with simple foot races. We tamed wild horses and then rode them in races. Desert people raced camels. The Romans raced chariots around the Colosseum.

Since then, humans have raced sailboats, bicycles, dogsleds, hot air balloons, and stagecoaches. We race down mountains on skis, bobsleds, and luges. Swimmers race across pools, lakes, and oceans.

People will race just about anything! Snowmobiles go fast in weather that is suitable for polar bears and penguins!

Once the engine was invented, racing really took off! Thrill seekers race all types of cars, trucks, motorcycles, motorboats, and airplanes.

These days, if it moves, we race it. And that's where wild racers come in. If a vehicle rolls and moves, someone is racing it somewhere.

People add motors to skateboards to make Go-Peds. Fun-loving drivers haul junk cars to racetracks and crash them into each other at demolition derbies. Dragsters shifted from cars to dump trucks and big rigs. Daredevil motorcycle riders zip around ice tracks on metal-spiked tires.

Snowmobiles were invented in the 1950s. At first, they were used by ski patrollers and other wintertime workers. But it wasn't long before snowmobiles were racing. Drivers took them around icy ovals, up mountainsides, and along snowy obstacle courses. Today, snowmobile drag racers even compete on grass and water!

Wild racers include motorized skateboards and pocket bikes, miniature versions of NASCAR (National Association for Stock Car Auto Racing) cars, motor homes, and sit-down lawn mowers. Let's take a fast spin through the world of Wild Racers!

It's not a giant riding a regular-sized motorcycle. It's a regular-sized man riding a pocket bike.

∎INSIDE STORY ▐▐▐▐▌

Ben-Hur Rides Again!

The thrilling chariot races in the 1959 movie *Ben-Hur* helped it win eleven Academy Awards. That ancient sport was as popular during the days of the Roman Empire as NASCAR is now. Today, tourists can cheer a reenactment of bygone chariot racing at a daily show staged in the Middle Eastern city of Jerash, Jordan. In the meantime, modern chariot racers compete every winter at events in some western states. The world championships are held in Ogden, Utah.

Wild racers have a long, odd, and funny history.

The first Indianapolis 500 was held on Memorial Day in 1911 at the Indianapolis Motor Speedway. Since then, the Indy 500 has become one of the most famous annual auto races in the world. Today, most of the **open-wheel** cars that are entered in the 500-mile (805-kilometer) event are pretty much the same. Over the years, some wilder entries have raced.

In fact, the very first winner, Ray Harroun, drove an oddity called the Marmon Wasp. It was the only single-seater in the race. The other thirty-nine racers drove two-seaters. They brought along their mechanics for the ride. The mechanics watched their own engines, as well as other racers nearby.

In 1946 veteran racer Paul Russo piloted a Fageol Twin Coach. It featured two engines and four-wheel drive. He crashed on the sixteenth lap.

Tank or car? Well, a little of both. This is one of only four Bugatti Type 32 tank cars. It was pretty good for racing, but not very comfortable!

Two years later the Indy 500's one-and-only six-wheeled car, the Pat Clancy Special, finished in twelfth place.

In 1964 the Hurst Floor Shift Special was perhaps the strangest car ever to show up at The Brickyard. (That's the nickname for the famous race track. It used to be paved with more than 3 million bricks!) In that wild racer, the driver sat in a sidecar-type **cockpit**. It was attached alongside a section containing the engine and fuel tank. It, however, crashed during a practice run.

Speaking of crashes, say hello to **demolition** derbies, another early type of wild race. Drivers crash their junk cars into one another until only one is left running. It's bumper cars for real. Most racing historians say the sport originated in the 1950s in Long Island, New York. The words *demolition derby* first appeared in a dictionary in 1953.

Ray Harroun's 1911 Marmon Wasp was a pioneer. A few years after he drove it, almost all the Indy-car drivers were riding solo.

∎INSIDE STORY ∥∥∥∥∥

Bugatti Type 32 Tank

Ettore Bugatti was an Italian race car designer. In 1909 he opened a factory in France that produced super-fast cars. He shocked the racing world in 1923 with the unusual Type 32. It was a short, boxy racer that became known as "The Tank." It was powered by an 8-cylinder engine and 3-speed transmission. Only four Type 32s were produced. They all were entered in that year's French Grand Prix. But only one finished the race, coming in third. That's not bad for a tank.

WRECKING CREWS

Today's demolition derby drivers destroy all types of vehicles.

Everyone likes to drive safely. When you don't, you can get in trouble with the law . . . and your doctor. But sometimes, drivers want to be free of trouble. That must explain the thrill drivers seek when they enter a demolition derby. Instead of trouble, they earn trophies and cash prizes for wrecking stuff.

These drivers have a blast, but they are still cautious. Even controlled car crashes can be dangerous. Drivers remove windshields, windows, lights, bumpers, and interior parts. Doors and trunk lids are welded shut. Gas tanks and batteries are bolted down. Add a funky paint job, and you're good to go wild.

In demolition (also called *demo*) derbies, accidents are supposed to happen. Fire crews stand by in case a battered car bursts into flames. Paramedics stand by to treat any injuries, and ambulances are at the scene for those who are seriously hurt. Tow trucks quickly haul broken vehicles off the track.

▮INSIDE STORY ▌▌▌▌▌▌

Demo TV

In the 1970s ABC's *Wide World of Sports* sometimes showed demolition derbies. Today you can find demo derbies on YouTube. Kids play demolition derby video games. In 2005–2006 Spike TV showed *Carpocalypse*. The title combines car and apocalypse, which means enormous destruction. Crash-happy racers competed in amazing demo derbies. They came up with Minivan Reverse Race, Blindfold Race, and Car Soccer. Some teams had to build a different crazy vehicle every episode—then wreck it! The series was a huge hit.

Demolition derby cars have all the glass removed. They keep going until they can't roll anymore.

Demo derby drivers have to wear helmets and seat belts. But when it comes to strategy, it's all about survival. The idea is to aim for and crash into as many cars as you can, but, at the same time, try to avoid becoming a victim yourself. Most derbies keep competitors circling a track, but backing up and going sideways is okay, too.

Drivers do more than wreck **sedans** and station wagons. So they have turned to—and turned over—pickup trucks, SUVs, and minivans. They've also smashed motor homes, riding lawn mowers, and farm machines. In fact, if it rolls, someone probably uses it in a demolition derby.

Derby drivers have to be able to smash into cars behind them as well as those in front of them.

SLIP 'N' SLIDE

The extreme motor sport of drift racing is fast, furious, and totally out of control.

The challenge in most car races is to keep the vehicle under control. In drift racing, the whole idea is to lose control.

Drift racing—or drifting—started in Japan during the 1990s. Daring drivers would steer their cars along curvy mountain roads. Instead of carefully going through turns, they would make their cars spin out. The cars would fishtail. That means that the back end of the car slides outward. Drivers used the brakes, the **clutch**, and skillful steering to prevent the car from going completely out of control.

Today, drifting is a hot **amateur** and professional motor sport in Japan, Europe, and the United States. Cars include special drifting engines, tires, and **suspensions**.

Drift racers make their cars go into skids around turns. The rear tires smoke as they try to grip the road.

Mini Drifters

Even if you don't have a driver's license, you can get into drifting. Radio-controlled (RC) cars have been popular with kids and adults for years. RC fans can buy small cars that look like full-size drifters. They come with drifting motors, tires, shocks, and brakes. They also have working lights and other real-life-like parts. RC drifting events are sometimes held alongside real drifting races.

Popular drifters include the Nissan 240SX, the Mazda RX-7, the Toyota AE86, the Pontiac Solstice, and the Ford Mustang.

Drifting isn't like traditional car races where the first to cross the finish line wins. Drivers are judged on style points, as in figure skating and diving. Judges award points and choose two cars for the finals. In the final, the lead car performs a series of drifts while the chase car tries to mess him up.

In side-by-side drift racing, two cars head into a corner at the same time. The winner will be the car that finishes high, but also shows a lot of style. That gets points from judges.

DAFFY DRAGSTERS

Move over, Funny Cars. Make room for drag racing dump trucks, big rigs, and other wild racers.

Dragsters can reach speeds of over 300 miles per hour (483 km/h). They can cover a quarter-mile (400 meters) in less than five seconds! Drag racing has a long and speedy history. In the 1930s hot rodders would race each other on long, flat stretches. They reached speeds of over 100 miles per hour (161 km/h). Organized drag racing got going in the late 1940s and 1950s.

Funny Cars are a type of dragster. They got their name from their unusual designs.

Big and fast! Drag racing fans are always looking for new ways to fill their need for speed. Large truck racing is one of the newest races.

The National Hot Rod Association (NHRA) runs most of today's drag races. The NHRA uses three basic types of dragsters—Top Fuel, Funny Car, and Pro Stock. Top Fuel cars are long and skinny. Funny Cars have wild, oversized bodies. Pro Stock cars look like cars you see on the street. All three go really fast over a short distance.

Yet, dragster trucks are a new, unofficial wrinkle in the sport. Pickup trucks are built with powerful engines and fancy paint jobs. But they're small compared to 18-wheel big rigs, with trailers hitched to them!

In drag races there is a stack of colored lights, known as a **Christmas Tree**. These lights signal the drivers when to take off. The big rigs don't get anywhere near 300 miles per hour (483 km/h). They do go pretty fast, though!

Other wild dragsters include giant dump trucks, tow trucks, and monster trucks. What's next? Maybe you'll see drag-racing tow trucks—hauling 18-wheelers!

■ INSIDE STORY ||||||

Truck Drags for Charity

Kids love puppies, ponies, and trucks! The bigger they are—the better. So, truck drag racing is the perfect event to attract kids and families. That's the thinking behind the Truckin' for Kids Truck Drags and Show & Shine. The daylong festivities are held every year at the Irwindale Speedway in Irwindale, California. More than 250 big rigs—of all makes and models, shapes and sizes—show up. Drivers show off their awesome trucks and drag-racing skills.

MINICUP CARS

They're half the size of NASCAR racers, but they measure a full pack of wild racing fun.

If you look at a minicup car race at a certain angle, you'd swear you were watching a NASCAR event. Yet, you'll quickly notice that the cars zooming around the track are exactly half the size of real stock cars. In racing, stock cars are the type used in NASCAR races. They look somewhat like passenger cars you might see on the street. But these stock cars are made just for racing.

Looks like a NASCAR race, right? But it's not! These are minicup cars, a training ground for drivers.

Minicups are miniature versions of cars used in NASCAR's Sprint Cup events. It's a very affordable form of car racing for beginners—minicups cost a fraction of the amount needed to buy a NASCAR racer. Every car is almost exactly the same, so races come down to who drives best. Because of the cars' size, minicup drivers as young as eight years old race in a youth division. The sport is run by the Miniature Motorsports Racing Association (MMRA).

Minicup cars are a great way for younger drivers like this boy to practice the skills of racing.

The group holds minicup races at half-mile (.80-km) tracks around the country.

All minicups are powered by a small engine. The **chassis** is made of steel tubes. The bodies are designed to look like real NASCAR models— Chevrolet Monte Carlo, Ford Taurus, Pontiac Grand Prix, and Dodge Intrepid.

Kids from eight to sixteen years old compete in Future Stars of Racing. Races last for fifty laps or thirty minutes, whichever comes first. The speeds aren't as fast as in real stock car racing, but the action is exciting. The winner is the first to cross under the **checkered flag**.

■INSIDE STORY ||||||

Growing Sport

Drivers over sixteen years old who outgrow minicups—and are fairly serious about moving up to stock cars someday—can bump up to MMRA's Baby Grand racing. The cars are two-thirds the size of Sprint Cup cars. They can top 100 miles per hour (161 km/h). Baby Grands race on NASCAR-style short tracks and road courses. Baby Grand races have been run at Daytona and other famous NASCAR venues.

MOTORIZED MARVELS

Hook up a little motor to a skateboard or a push scooter and hang on for some big-time, fast-moving, feet-free fun.

Skateboards have come a long way from boards on wheels. The first skateboards came along in the 1960s. In the beginning a skateboard was a pair of roller-skate wheels nailed to a surfboard-shaped slab of wood. It was rough riding, but still fun. Softer wheels came along to smooth the ride. Today, kids ride millions of awesome skateboards. Short and long boards are used to do all kinds of amazing tricks.

Up, up, and away! This is not a bunch of guys, but just one. Several photos were combined to capture this daredevil doing a backflip on a scooter.

All those tricks are done without motors. But some skaters wanted to put some power behind their board. They figured out ways to attach a motor to their skateboard! Now you can find minimotors that are either gas- or electric-powered. Some motorized boards will whip along at 20 miles per hour (32 km/h)—no foot-pushing needed.

Scooters have been around for a long time—but not as racers. The first scooters were clunky wooden things. In the 1990s modern aluminum scooters with folding handles changed scooters forever.

Guess what? Folks have added motors to scooters, too! The steering makes them easier to handle, so you'll find bigger motors on scooters. Some will go 45 miles per hour (72 km/h)!

One of the most popular types is the Go-Ped. It was invented in California in 1985 by Steve Patmont. The Go-Ped comes in many styles and prices. For example, a deluxe, battery-powered electric model called the Hoverboard sells for nearly three thousand dollars!

The engine (the red block) on a motor scooter powers the rear wheel.

INSIDE STORY ||||||

Go-Pedders Gone Wild!

Go-Ped lovers have taken their rides to the track. They wear motorcycle-style safety helmets, knee pads, and elbow pads. They run lap or drag races. They also take part in scootercross. As in BMX (bicycle motocross) and motorcycle **motocross**, riders go over jumps, tight turns, and other obstacles. There are even go-pedders who customize their rides with knobby tires and go off-road racing.

POCKET ROCKETS

Small, but fast! That describes the crazy new sport of pocket bike racing.

Sometimes smaller is better. A pocket bike (also called a minimoto or a pitbike) is a miniature motorcycle. It's about one-quarter the size of a motorcycle you might see on the road, but looks a lot like the real thing.

Pocket bikes look like superbikes that are used by pro riders. The superbikes can go well over 100 miles per hour (161 km/h). Pocket bikes have small, gas-powered engines. They can go from 20 miles per hour (32 km/h) up to around 60 miles per hour (97 km/h). Brand-new pocket bikes can cost as little as two hundred to three hundred dollars. Fancier models can cost thousands of dollars.

Adults look sort of silly on pocket bikes. Imagine Papa Bear on Goldilocks's teensy tricycle. Pocket bikes are just right for kids. Safety comes first, no matter what you ride. Always wear full-face helmets, goggles, padded gloves, long shirts, pants, and knee and elbow pads.

Pocket-bike riders have to be very flexible. They have to keep their knees bent for a long time during races.

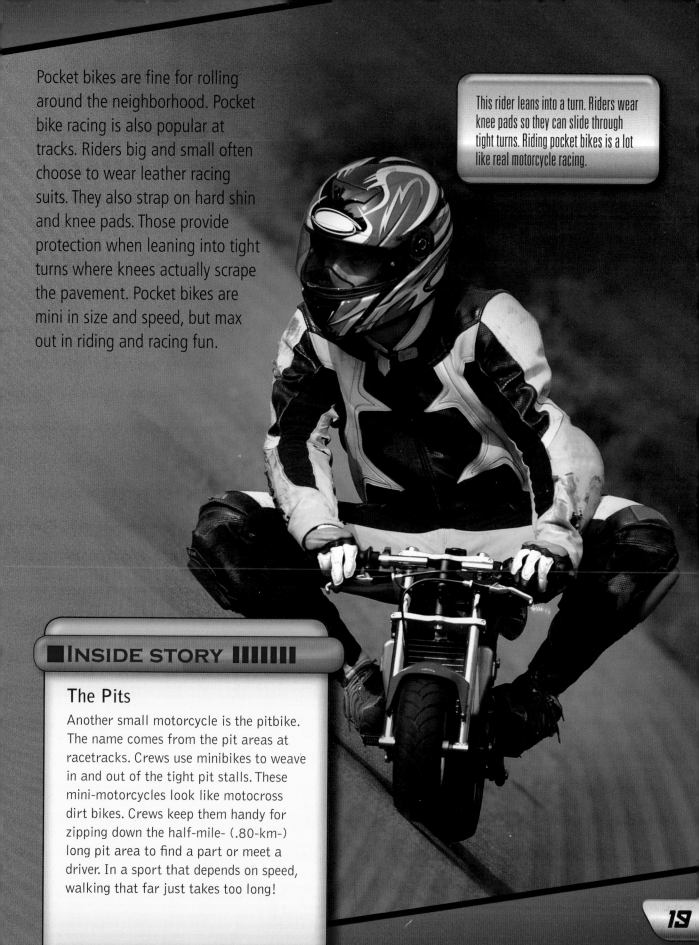

Pocket bikes are fine for rolling around the neighborhood. Pocket bike racing is also popular at tracks. Riders big and small often choose to wear leather racing suits. They also strap on hard shin and knee pads. Those provide protection when leaning into tight turns where knees actually scrape the pavement. Pocket bikes are mini in size and speed, but max out in riding and racing fun.

This rider leans into a turn. Riders wear knee pads so they can slide through tight turns. Riding pocket bikes is a lot like real motorcycle racing.

▮INSIDE STORY ▌▌▌▌▌▌

The Pits

Another small motorcycle is the pitbike. The name comes from the pit areas at racetracks. Crews use minibikes to weave in and out of the tight pit stalls. These mini-motorcycles look like motocross dirt bikes. Crews keep them handy for zipping down the half-mile- (.80-km-) long pit area to find a part or meet a driver. In a sport that depends on speed, walking that far just takes too long!

RIDE ON THE WILD SIDE

Motorcycle racing is exciting all by itself. Add sidecars and the action is twice as thrilling.

Motorcycles are fun, but only hold one person. That's where the idea of attaching a sidecar to a motorcycle came from.

A sidecar is a seat attached to the side of a motorcycle. It has a single rear wheel that lines up with the rear wheel of the motorcycle. Besides carrying an extra passenger, sidecars also are handy for hauling stuff. Military motorcycles with sidecars were widely used during World War II. A driver could deliver a messenger or carry a passenger to another place.

These odd three-wheelers found a place in the wild racing world. The driver controls the motorcycle. A teammate in the sidecar shifts his weight in turns to keep the speeding vehicle from tipping over. World championships in sidecar racing have been held since 1949.

By the 1960s racing teams began using streamlined fiberglass moldings on the motorcycles and sidecars to make them more aerodynamic. Those evolved into today's sleek, specialized road rockets.

Attending a sidecar race is amazing. You'll enjoy the speed of the motorcycles. You'll also marvel at the balance and bravery of the passenger!

The sidecar rider is not falling out, he's balancing the bike.

Sidecar racing can be wild and muddy.

Moto Tandems

Motocross motorcycle racing is very popular. Crowds cheer as brave bikers bounce over dirt-covered obstacle courses. Sidecar-cross has also caught on. The driver does his best to keep the bike and sidecar speeding along the course. In the meantime, the passenger stands, kneels, leans, and climbs around. They work together to keep the motorcycle upright.

GET A GRIP

Motorcycle racing on ice? Sounds like trouble, but turns out it's fun!

Ice is very slippery. It's hard to walk on. But people have found lots of ways to move on it. Metal skate blades help hockey players, speed skaters, and figure skaters easily slide on ice. Long, blade-like runners support ice sailboats on frozen lakes and rivers. Tracks on snowmobiles grip the surface during ice oval races. Olympians race down icy chutes on bobsleds and luges.

Rubber motorcycle tires aren't much good on ice, though. But that hasn't stopped wild racers! They started out by simply sticking metal screws into tires. Today, extreme motorcycle ice racing is done on both indoor and outdoor tracks. It is a huge international motor sport. Spiked tires dig deep into the ice to hold tight at speeds of up to 60 miles per hour (97 km/h).

The motorcycles themselves look like dirt bikes. Most have only one or two gears and no brakes. Generally, each bike has ninety spikes on the front tire and between two hundred and five hundred on the rear one. To make races fair, everyone must use the same type of spikes.

Outdoor ice racing is a popular wintertime sport in Europe, Canada, and the United States.

Ice motorcycle racers wear lots of protective gear. With knee braces and the metal spikes on the tires, they can lean over very far.

The American Motorcyclist Association (AMA) runs pro indoor ice racing events throughout the United States. Another indoor pro series is organized by International Championship Events (ICE). In ICE events the bikes have large engines and a rear brake. Racers rip around oval tracks for four laps. The ice is always cold and slippery, but the action is hot!

▮INSIDE STORY ▮▮▮▮▮▮

More Wheels on Ice

Cars have been racing on ice for a while. All-terrain vehicles (ATVs) and go-karts with spiked tires have also gone ice racing. In 2009 ICE started a division for pitbikes. Riders in those races must be at least sixteen years old and wear safety gear. Their gas-powered pitbikes have a spiked front tire no more than 12 inches (30 centimeters) in diameter and a 10-inch (25-cm) rear tire.

THE WILD SIDE OF SNOWMOBILING

Snowmobiles started out as work vehicles. Now sled heads work hard at racing them—and not just on snow!

Snow has always been a lot of fun to play in. Working in the freezing-cold snow used to be tough. Years ago, ranchers had a hard time getting food to hungry livestock. It was hard for loggers to reach trees in snow-covered forests. Ski patrollers battled deep snow while searching for lost skiers.

Those important jobs and many others got a whole lot easier in 1959. That's when Canadian inventor Joseph-Armand Bombardier introduced the Ski-Doo snowmobile. The machines quickly became a useful and fun rides.

By the early 1970s more than 2 million snowmobilers rode through snowy fields and groomed trails. By then, the sport of snowmobile racing was off and running.

Some people just take snowmobiles out for a nice ride in the forest— the racing comes later!

Today's snowmobiles have front skis, snow-gripping tracks, and powerful engines. Snowmobiles can cut through the deepest drifts or zoom across frozen lakes. They can even climb steep mountainsides covered with fresh powder.

The snowmobile quickly became a useful and fun machine. By the early 1970s more than 2 million snowmobilers rode through snowy fields and groomed trails. By then, the sport of snowmobile racing was off and running.

Meanwhile, snowmobile racers come in many models. Some have huge engines and extra-wide tracks for scrambling up mountainsides. Light and powerful models are set up for rough riding in snocross—snowmobiling's motocross-type event. Some machines are perfect for extreme flips, twists, and other airborne tricks. They're used in freestyle events. The sleds in ice oval events run on tracks with extra-deep teeth.

■ INSIDE STORY ▮▮▮▮▮▮

Off on the Right Track

Snowmobiling is a great family activity. Even preschoolers can become snowmobile riders. They ride pint-sized models with small engines and smaller-than-normal tracks, handlebars, and seats. These machines are the snowy version of pocket bikes. Kids from four to ten years old race on larger and larger snowmobiles in longer and longer races.

Rubber tracks

Big teeth on rubber tracks dig into the snow ... or help snowmobiles get some air!

25

DASHING THROUGH THE SNOW

Snocross racers fly over bumps and jumps like Santa's reindeer.

The extreme sport of snocross is similar to motocross racing on motorcycles. The difference is that the race is on snow instead of dirt. In snocross, racers battle one another along an outdoor course. They ride through tight turns and banked corners. They zip over steep jumps and tricky obstacles. Of course, everything's covered with snow. Snocross is a flurry of fun.

Snocross racers choose performance-style snowmobiles. That means the snowmobiles are designed for high speeds and rugged riding. Some types can reach 60 miles per hour (97 km/h) or more on the tracks. A lightweight hood covers the engine. Short racing handlebars control the pair of skis in front. The skis are attached to adjustable shock absorbers, which soften landings over jumps.

▮INSIDE STORY ▌▌▌▌▌▌

Head for the Hills

One of the things that makes wild racing so wild is the never-ending search for new events or twists on old ones. That's the attitude snowmobilers had when they combined elements of snocross and hill climbs to come up with hillcross. Groups of six riders race up a ski-hill course filled with sharp turns through gates, humpy moguls, rapid series of washboard bumps, and other obstacles. Riders reach speeds of over 70 miles per hour (113 km/h), while trying to maneuver the course and avoid crashing into other racers. The first sled to the top wins.

Deep snow is no problem for snowmobiles. They can dig through powder, zoom over ice, or slip in and out of snowy forests.

Performance snowmobiles are the best around. New models range from $6,000 to $12,000. They include heated hand grips and seats, digital gauges, racing mirrors, and sporty windshields.

There are snocross races for amateur riders of different ages and skill levels. Kids from seven to seventeen years old can find a place to race. It's no surprise that most races—and snowmobiles—are found in the northern United States. That's where winters are long, cold, and snowy. Snocross is popular in Michigan, Minnesota, New York, and Wisconsin, to name a few states.

KING OF THE HILL

Snowmobile hill climbs challenge racers to battle super-steep courses—and gravity!

Skiers and snowboarders compete in thrilling races to see who can get down a mountainside the fastest. On other hills, snowmobilers go the other way. They're trying to post the fastest time up to the top of a snowy course.

Each snowmobile hill climb is challenging. One course might run fairly straight up a pretty steep but gentle hill. Another course might follow a zigzag route over rough and dangerous land. It could go for thousands of feet to the top of an icy, rocky mountain.

Down the hill he goes! Whether following in the tracks of other racers or creating new trails, downhill racers need courage and speed.

In 1976 a wild-and-crazy bunch of racers claim to have launched the sport in Jackson Hole, Wyoming. They had been bragging about who could ride their snowmobile fastest to the top of 7,800-foot (2,377-meter) Snow King Mountain. Today, the annual World Championship Snowmobile Hill Climb draws more than 250 courageous international competitors. The race course starts at the bottom of a long ski trail. Racers have to weave in and out of fifteen gates. Some treacherous sections are on skiers' **black-diamond runs**. Only half of the competitors make it to the summit—in less than a minute. The other half fall or get bounced off their sleds. Unmanned sleds tumble down the mountain. They are a danger to fans and racers alike!

■INSIDE STORY ■IIIIII

Custom Climbers

Hill climbers use special snowmobiles. The engines are more powerful to conquer the steep hills. The sleds are also lighter. That makes them easier to power uphill. The tracks and runners are wider as well. That lets the snowmobile grip the snow better and defeat the forces of gravity. Of course, the most important part of the uphill snowmobile is the brave driver!

Flat stretches let riders gain ground on the drivers ahead of them . . . or rest a bit from the gravity!

Some snowmobile races are like NASCAR, driving around frozen, circular tracks.

The oldest and fastest type of snowmobile competition is called ice oval racing. The races are held on outdoor circular tracks, packed hard with ice and snow. Groups of snowmobile drivers line up at the start. An official waves a green flag. They're off! Racers try to stay at the front of the pack. To get there, they have to pass other drivers. At the end of the race, the first sled across the finish line is the winner.

Snowmobile racers gather at the starting line. The course quickly narrows after the start. Getting a jump on the other drivers is key.

Organized races started back in the mid–1960s. Amateur events for adults and kids have been held since. Those races give weekend warriors a great chance to test their skills in a safe setting.

In the meantime, pro ice oval racing has become a big-time winter sport. Adults and teenage racers compete in different divisions. The pros' sleds can reach over 100 miles per hour (161 km/h)! The snowmobile tracks have spikes (also called studs) to help grip the ice. Because racers circle the course while turning left, the left-hand ski is made from extra-tough material.

One of the most famous ice oval events has been held every winter since 1964 in Wisconsin. The Eagle River World Championship Snowmobile Derby is a ten-day festival that welcomes thousands of fans and racers. There are three days of old-time races featuring classic sleds. Those are followed by snocross and ice oval races. It's all simply good, clean, fast, snowy fun.

Here's a good look at the rubber teeth and metal gears that make up a snowmobile track.

■INSIDE STORY ‖‖‖‖‖

Geared Up for Safety

Snowmobile racers—adults, kids, amateurs, and pros—always wear safety equipment. Full-face motorcycle-type helmets are often orange to stand out against white ice and snow. Goggles or other eye protection is worn underneath. A thick, windproof jacket and pants, or a one-piece snowmobiling suit, keeps a racer cozy. Padded gloves and shin guards are important. Feet stay dry, warm, and protected inside heavy boots that cover the ankles.

Freestyle snowmobiling is about as wild as you can get.

Many racing fans have seen riders zoom off a ramp and catch some air. They can do this on a skateboard, a bicycle, or even a motorcycle. What about racing on a 500-pound (227-kilogram) snowmobile? Now that's an extreme sport!

Freestyle snowmobile riders are always looking for new thrills and chills. They ride light, quick sleds down a short runway that leads to a snow-packed jump. In the air, they turn, twist, and stretch their bodies in all sorts of directions. They do all that while keeping control of the snowmobile. But the ultimate move is putting the airborne sled into a complete, 360-degree back flip. That's totally sick, as freestylers like to say. After all that, they try to land safely on the sled as the crowd cheers.

Smush! A freestyle rider lands and kicks up a huge cloud of powdery snow. Riders need to learn how to land safely after they complete their tricks.

One hand, no feet! Freestyle riders do amazing tricks.

Judges grade freestylers on their style, plus their success in sticking their mid air acrobatics. Sticking means landing safely after doing a trick really well. Some of the jumps are more than 100-feet (30-m) long. Those can send a rider and snowmobile more than 30 feet (9 m) off the ground. That's as high as a three-story building! It's not hard to imagine how skilled—and a bit nutty—freestylers have to be.

■INSIDE STORY ▌▌▌▌▌▌

X, as in Extreme

ESPN's X Games have become the Olympics of extreme sports. X Games athletes compete for gold, silver, and bronze medals. At the Winter X Games, medals are awarded in snowboarding, freestyle skiing, and snowmobiling events. In 2009 the Winter X Games 13, held in Aspen, Colorado, featured a new snowmobile event, called best trick. Only three athletes were chosen to compete. Each took two jumps that were judged by fans at the event and those watching on TV.

NO SNOW? NO PROBLEM!

People race snowmobiles even in places where there isn't any snow.

Some wild snowmobilers just can't get enough. They hate the end of winter because that means no more snowmobiling. Good news! Who needs snow when you can drag race your snowmobile on a paved strip? How about grass? The National Hot Rod Association (NHRA) has added snowmobile drags to many national and regional events.

A drag-racing sled has a rubberized track. It also has front skis with wheels and another set of wheels on the back. It has a part that helps to cool everything down after a race.

Drag-racing snowmobiles can really move! Winning times on a quarter-mile (400 m) asphalt track have been clocked at a little over eight seconds, with speeds topping 150 miles per hour (241 km/h)!

Drag racing on grassy strips requires different gear. The rubber track has spikes (studs) in it for better traction on grass. Neither the track nor the skis have wheels attached to them. The times and speeds may not be nearly as fast as on asphalt, but non-winter fun on a snowmobile is always a moving experience.

No snow? No problem! Snowmobiles can be adapted for use on the calm, wave-free water of lakes and rivers.

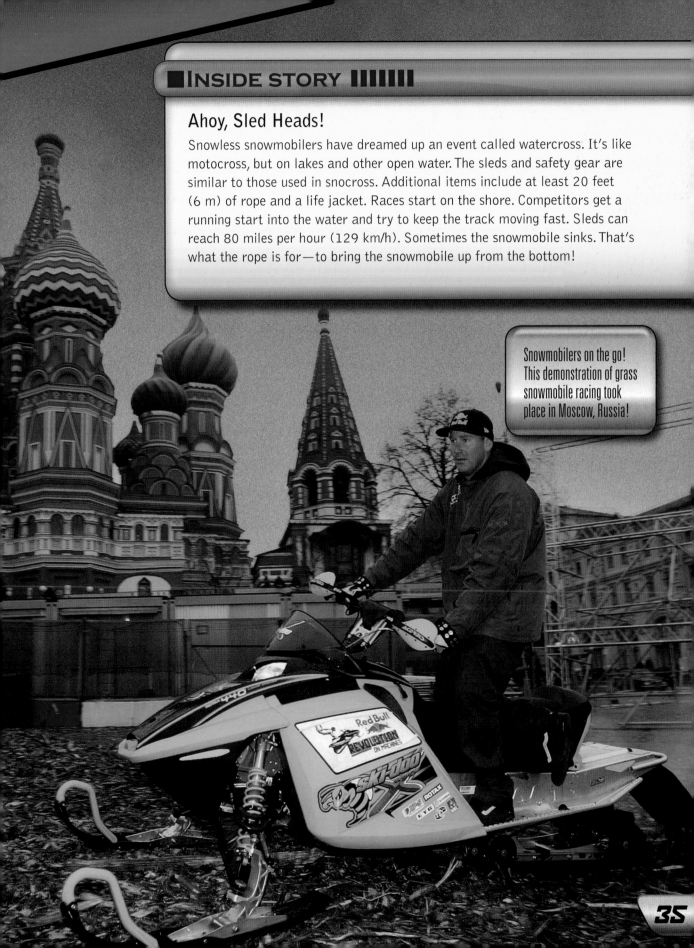

Ahoy, Sled Heads!

Snowless snowmobilers have dreamed up an event called watercross. It's like motocross, but on lakes and other open water. The sleds and safety gear are similar to those used in snocross. Additional items include at least 20 feet (6 m) of rope and a life jacket. Races start on the shore. Competitors get a running start into the water and try to keep the track moving fast. Sleds can reach 80 miles per hour (129 km/h). Sometimes the snowmobile sinks. That's what the rope is for—to bring the snowmobile up from the bottom!

Snowmobilers on the go! This demonstration of grass snowmobile racing took place in Moscow, Russia!

GRASS-ROOTS RACING

Ladies and gentlemen, start your lawn mowers!

It's one thing to mow your lawn in a hurry. It's quite another to hurry on your lawn mower. That means racing a lawn mower to the finish line—at speeds of over 60 miles per hour (97 km/h)! Instead of cutting the grass, these wild racers are on the cutting edge of *mow*torsports

Lawn mower racing traces its roots to England in 1973. A race car driver named Jim Gavin wanted to come up with a new type of racing that anyone could try. As he wondered what vehicle to race, he looked out the window. He saw a man cutting the grass on a riding lawn mower. Presto! Lawn mower racing was born.

Nearly twenty years later the sport was imported to the United States by the makers of Sta-Bil. This is a product added to gasoline to make engines run better. It started as a fun way to help sell more Sta-Bil. Now it has become the U.S. Lawn Mower Racing Association (USLMRA).

The racing machines start out as everyday riding mowers. Drivers remove the cutting blade and keep the original mower skeleton. Then, changes are made to the engine, tires, and body. The races are held on oval dirt tracks.

The rubber tires are used to show the racers where to go on the course. The tires also help soften the fall if riders tip over!

There are races for adults and for kids as young as ten years old. To start a race, drivers dash to their machines, start their engines, and take off. The best way to watch a race? Sitting in a lawn chair.

Where's the lawn for these mowers? Lawn mowers don't usually race on grass, but on dirt. Thick tires on the machines help dig into the dirt.

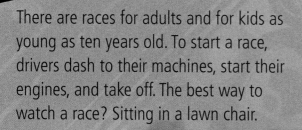

▮INSIDE STORY ▮▮▮▮▮▮

Vid-e-Mow Game

Don't have a lawn to mow? Try the Lawn Mower Racing Mania 2007 video game. Challenge racers such as Angelina Mowlie, Sodzilla, Weedy Gonzales, and Geronimow. Choose from eighteen different racetracks, including Wally's Wild Oval, Turfmaster Classic, and Shantytown Mowdown. Customize your mower. Lean into turns. When you're done, go outside and mow the real lawn!

Burning Man is an annual art event held in the Nevada desert. Among the craziest sights are Mutant Vehicles.

Every summer the Burning Man party happens in the flat, dry Black Rock Desert in northern Nevada. The first Burning Man was held in San Francisco in 1986. The highlight was when an 8-foot-tall (2-m-tall) wooden statue of a man was set on fire to celebrate the **summer solstice**.

These days, nearly 50,000 artists and creative people from around the world blaze a trail to Burning Man. They establish a tent-filled Black Rock City. The organizers establish a different theme every year. Artists make all kinds of objects to display. A highlight is still the traditional Saturday-night burning of the wooden man.

It's not racing, but this unique creation is one of the many Art Cars that are part of the Burning Man festival.

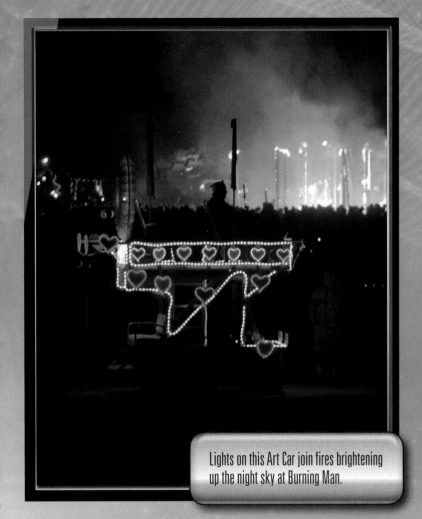

Lights on this Art Car join fires brightening up the night sky at Burning Man.

Art Cars on Parade

Wildly designed and decorated vehicles are not found only at Burning Man. Artists also put together all kinds of movable contraptions. You may see them driving around in public or on display at car shows and parades. The annual Houston Art Car Parade claims to be the world's largest and oldest such event. Nearly three hundred unique creations with wheels are entered in a competition to win money and trophies. The event also doubles as a fund-raiser for local charities.

Art Cars or Mutant Vehicles are the most colorful, bizarre, and one-of-a-kind moving objects. Some are everyday cars, trucks, or motorcycles. They are painted and decorated. Others are built completely from scratch. Owners must prove that their vehicles are safe—as well as crazy.

Burning Man artists have decorated fire trucks, school buses, scooters, golf carts, and every other type of moving thing with wheels. They've been made to look like pirate ships, rockets, living rooms, fish, and ponies. On the roads in Black Rock, you might see giant insects, cats, couches, lobsters, giant heads, or flying saucers. Many light up at night. Mutant Vehicle parades and races often break out. Then, as with everything in Black Rock City, they all disappear without a trace, until the next Burning Man.

ALL GEARED UP

The British TV show *Top Gear* is usually serious about reviewing cars. Sometimes the hosts go crazy.

Buying a $200,000 Italian sports car is serious business. You want to get the right information before you spend big money. The auto experts who host the British TV show *Top Gear* offer just that—and a little more. Hosts for the show are Jeremy, Richard, James, and the mysterious Stig. Every episode, they check out the latest car models. They drive cars from Ferrari, BMW, Nissan, Aston Martin, and Chevrolet. Celebrity guests often join them. The show offers great information and it's a lot of fun.

The hosts like to get silly once in a while. They might do a motorcycle jump over a bunch of mini-motor homes. They play car soccer, with two cars knocking around a giant soccer ball. Once they even set up an off-road race between an army tank and a Range Rover.

Car Darts, Anyone?

Top Gear launched one of the wildest car events ever. The hosts remembered spy movies in which cars flew through the air. They decided to try it out. They took some junk cars to a high cliff. At the bottom of the cliff, they painted a gigantic target. Then they took turns aiming flying cars at the target below. It was like car darts! The show's biggest laughs came when they added a challenge: hit a motor home parked in the bull's-eye. Crash!

One of the wilder *Top Gear* stunts was motor-home racing. Richard's idea was to use vehicles that fans normally take to car races—motor homes—and race them instead. He lined up a half dozen old motor homes and their drivers. He even made up a set of ridiculous rules for his new motor sport.

For example, you had to be able to drive your motor home to the track. The racers also could not bump or run into each other. Well, the fifteen-lap race didn't exactly go by the rules. It actually turned into a crazy demolition derby. By the end the track was littered with bits and pieces of the motor homes. Driving any of them home was impossible! The *Top Gear* guys won't try that with a fancy Mercedes!

Head to head, or should we say wheel to track! The crazy guys at the *Top Gear* TV show once matched up a tank like this one (left) and a powerful off-road Range Rover like this one (below) in a duel in the dirt. The Range Rover won for speed ... but the tank won for power!

FORMULA FOR SPEED

One of the wildest—and fastest—types of auto racing in the world is Formula One.

Americans enjoy different sports than people in Europe. For example, we love baseball and football. Europeans love cricket and soccer, which they call football. When it comes to auto racing in the United States, NASCAR is king. In Europe, Formula One—often shortened to F1—rules. Formula is the word for the official set of rules that all drivers and cars have to follow. One means the races with the best cars.

Auto racing in Europe dates back to the 1890s. Speeds then topped out at only 30 miles per

Here's a look at the twists and turns of a typical F1 race.

hour (48 km/h). The pace picked up in the first half of the twentieth century, but after World War II, racing really took off across Europe.

The first F1 race was held in England in 1950. F1 became a series of individual races, called Grand Prix, that today are held on road courses in many different countries.

F1 road courses are not ovals as in NASCAR. They're longer and include S-shaped curves, banked (tilted) corners, and straightaways. Open-wheel F1 race cars reach speeds of over 220 miles per hour (354 km/h). Grand Prix events average less than 200 miles (322 km) in length and are limited to two hours.

∎ INSIDE STORY ‖‖‖‖

First F1 Winner

Italian driver Nino Farina won the first F1 race in 1950. He won two more races that year. Those wins gave him F1's first world championship. He was a member of the Alfa Romeo racing team and drove a single-seat Alfa 158. It had a 200-**horsepower** (hp) engine with eight cylinders. Farina became famous for the way he sat in his race car. He kept low in the seat, with both arms stretched out straight.

There are seventeen Grand Prix races in the F1 series. The season starts in March, with the Australian Grand Prix. It wraps up in November in Abu Dhabi, the capital of the United Arab Emirates. Grand Prix races also are held in France, England, Germany, Italy, China, Turkey, Japan, and Brazil, among others.

In the United States, F1 isn't very big. But the sport is enormously popular in the rest of the world. Its drivers are international superstars.

F1 race cars are very low to the ground. This helps drivers keep control while going at high speed.

SUPER CAR

An F1 race car is built for one thing only—speed.

The chassis is the key part. An F1 chassis is made from light, but extremely strong plastic-like materials. At the center of the chassis is an open cockpit, where the driver sits. Open means it doesn't have a roof or windows. The car's powerful engine is behind the cockpit. It kicks out nearly 900 hp. Compare an F1 car to the 550-hp engine in a Corvette or a Mustang. Both those sporty American cars are among the fastest on the road. An F1 racer would leave them in the dust.

An F1 car has a horizontal wing on the front. It has another on the back. The wings act to push the speeding racer down. The big, thick tires on an F1 car also help the driver keep it under control. They're especially useful in tight turns. Like dragster tires, they have no treads. F1 slicks are made from soft rubber that heats up and sticks to the track. That's part of the formula that makes F1 the favorite motor sport of millions of racing fans.

Wild racers zoom around tracks, trails, and mountains. Racing any machine demands skill and daring. Racing any wild machine takes a little bit extra. Wild racers bring their imagination—and spirit—to every race.

Hot young British driver Lewis Hamilton became the first black F1 champion in 2008.

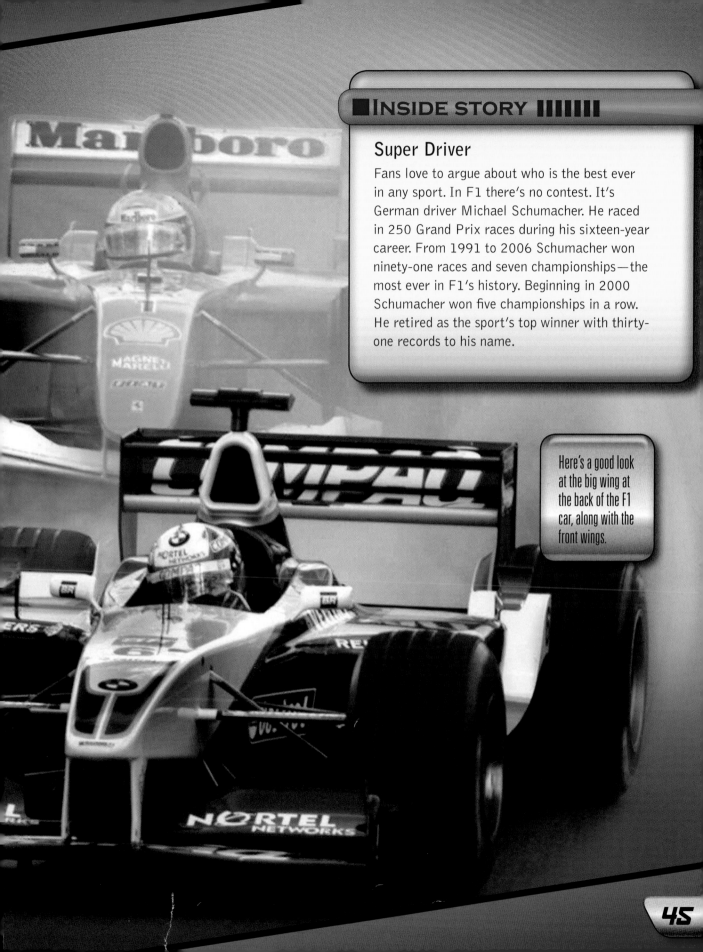

Super Driver

Fans love to argue about who is the best ever in any sport. In F1 there's no contest. It's German driver Michael Schumacher. He raced in 250 Grand Prix races during his sixteen-year career. From 1991 to 2006 Schumacher won ninety-one races and seven championships—the most ever in F1's history. Beginning in 2000 Schumacher won five championships in a row. He retired as the sport's top winner with thirty-one records to his name.

Here's a good look at the big wing at the back of the F1 car, along with the front wings.

GLOSSARY

amateur   A person who plays a sport without being paid.

black-diamond runs   Very difficult paths on a ski slope, marked by or signed with black diamonds.

chassis   The metal skeleton of a car.

checkered flag   The black-and-white flag waved over the winner of a motor race.

Christmas Tree   A metal pole with colored lights used to start a drag race.

clutch   A car part that controls the gears.

cockpit   The place where a driver sits in a race vehicle.

demolition   Destruction.

horsepower   A way of measuring the power of an engine.

motocross   A type of motorcycle race that takes place on rugged dirt tracks.

open-wheel   A type of race car that does not have fenders covering the tires.

sedan   A larger type of car with four doors.

summer solstice   The longest day of the year, when summer begins.

suspension   The parts of a car that control its up and down movement.

FIND OUT MORE

BOOKS

Finn, Denny. *Snowmobiling: Torque!* Eden Prairie, MN: Bellwether Media, 2009. Learn more about snowmobile touring, racing, and machines.

Hammond, Richard. *Car Science*. New York: DK Publishing, 2008. Peek inside the engines and other parts of racing machines of all sorts, from NASCAR racers to dragsters to drifters.

Streissguth, Thomas. *Pocket Bikes: Torque!* Eden Prairie, MN: Bellwether Media, 2009. A whole book on pocket bikes! This book is probably about as big as the seat on a pocket-bike . . . but it shows all about these mini-marvels.

WEBSITES

Visit these websites for more information:

www.formula1.com

This is the official site of Formula One. Check out stories about the drivers, read about the history of the sport, and keep up on the latest results.

www.nhra.com

The National Hot Rod Association (NHRA) sponsors racing for all kinds of wild machines, from Funny Cars and Top Fuel dragsters to snowmobile dragsters.

INDEX